Arthur Crawshay Alliston Hall

The Words from and to the Cross Meditations for Holy Week and Good Friday

Arthur Crawshay Alliston Hall

The Words from and to the Cross Meditations for Holy Week and Good Friday

ISBN/EAN: 9783337253561

Printed in Europe, USA, Canada, Australia, Japan

Cover: Foto ©Lupo / pixelio.de

More available books at **www.hansebooks.com**

THE WORDS
FROM AND TO THE CROSS

Meditations
FOR HOLY WEEK AND GOOD FRIDAY

BY

REV. A. C. A. HALL
MISSION PRIEST OF THE SOCIETY OF S. JOHN THE EVANGELIST

NEW YORK
JAMES POTT & CO., PUBLISHERS
14 AND 16 ASTOR PLACE
1891

PREFACE.

THE Meditations in this book were given in the Mission Church of S. John the Evangelist, Boston; those on the words spoken by our Lord from the Cross, at the Three Hours' Service on Good Friday, 1890; those on the words spoken to or of Him on the Cross, on the other days of Holy Week, 1888.

The Author ventures to think that in both courses of Meditations a somewhat wider range of thought and application is taken than is usual in such addresses, while at the same time an harmonious view of the Passion in some of its many aspects is preserved.

MISSION HOUSE OF S. JOHN EVANGELIST, BOSTON.
EPIPHANY, 1891.

CONTENTS.

HOLY WEEK MEDITATIONS.

The Words Addressed to our Lord on the Cross.

	PAGE
INTRODUCTORY	7
I. THE WORD OF ACCUSATION	11
II. THE WORD OF DERISION AND SCOFFING	21
III. THE WORD OF PRAYER	29
IV. THE WORD OF MISUNDERSTANDING	38
V. THE WORD OF ACKNOWLEDGMENT	46

GOOD FRIDAY MEDITATIONS.

The Seven Words Spoken by our Lord from the Cross.

FIRST WORD: THE TRUE REGARD OF SINNERS	53
SECOND WORD: OF PENITENTS	56
THIRD WORD: OF FRIENDS	60
FOURTH WORD: OF SIN	63
FIFTH WORD: OF PAIN	67
SIXTH WORD: OF WORK	71
SEVENTH WORD: GOD'S REGARD OF MAN AND MAN'S OF GOD	75

INTRODUCTORY.

1. In a hymn of Dr. Neale's for All Saints,[1] written shortly before his death, he turns to the different choirs of the Saints—the Martyrs, Confessors, Virgins, Doctors—asking of each the means by which they attained their sanctity and fulfilled their several vocations. The reply of each group is of course, in effect, Through Christ that strengthened us; He was in us the hope of glory, the power of victory. The Doctors, the great champions of the Faith, are begged to tell us how the lore to gain, by which they established the Truth, and crushed down heresy amain. This is their answer:

> "In the Cross we found our pulpit,
>   In the Seven Great Words our lore;
> Dying gift of dying Master,
>   Which once uttered all was o'er;
> Pillars seven of sevenfold wisdom,
>   Sion's safeguard evermore."

---

[1] "Christ's own martyrs, valiant cohort," in *Original Hymns and Sequences*, by Rev. J. M. Neale, D.D. (Hayes.)

It is somewhat in this light that I would ask you this Good Friday to listen to the Words of our Lord from the Cross, as declaring the true regard—God's and man's—of the chief objects that we have to meet in the world, the things and persons with which we have to do: Sinners, Penitents, Friends, Sin, Pain, Work. The true regard of each of these we will try to learn, viewed from the stand-point of the Cross.

2. God's view and man's, I say. Jesus is God and man. Ever from the moment of the Incarnation, as He lay cradled all lowly in Bethlehem, or in Mary's arms, or stretched on the hard bed of the Cross, we worship Him as true God and true Man. He is the Word made flesh, God of the essence of the Father, revealed in human flesh, showing forth the Divine perfections, translating them into language—the language of action—intelligible to us, declaring and making known the invisible God.[1] And Man He is of the substance of His mother, the ideal, pattern man, the true Representative of Humanity. Our Lord as the Incarnate Word, the Son of God and the Son of Man, is the revelation at once of what God is, and of what man, made in God's image, should be. The centurion's exclamation declared the

---
[1] S. John i. 14; 2 Cor. iv. 4.

truth, a fuller truth than he recognized, Truly this was God's Son, a Righteous Man.[1] From Him we would learn, and from His utterances on the Cross unspeakably solemn. All bare witness to His gracious words. None ever spake like this Man.

3. For what purpose do we listen to these Words? That we may arm ourselves with the same mind. Out of the abundance of the heart the mouth speaketh. We would learn His mind. We gather round the Cross not for the stirring of idle sentiment, nor to offer sympathy. We would not listen, and smite our breasts and return. We would render the homage of our obedience. We would hear these Words, and keep them, and do them. Not do the same things. We do not expect to be in the same circumstances; we are never likely to be exposed to bodily torture. But we would arm ourselves with the same mind that was in Christ Jesus.[2]

---

[1] S. Mark xv. 39; S. Luke xxiii. 47.
[2] 1 S. Pet. iv. 1.

HOLY WEEK MEDITATIONS.

The Words Spoken to, or of, our Lord on the Cross.

I.

THE WORD OF ACCUSATION.

"This is Jesus the King of the Jews."—S. MATTHEW xxvii. 37.

As on Good Friday we are accustomed to listen to and ponder on the Words spoken by our Blessed Lord *from* the Cross, so during this Holy Week let us meditate on the Words spoken *to* or *of* our Lord as He hangs upon the Cross. Five such sayings there are, each distinct from the others, each uttered by different persons or classes of persons.

1. *The Word of Accusation*—the Title written by Pilate: "This is Jesus the King of the Jews."

2. *The Word of Taunt and Scoffing*—uttered by the Chief Priests: "He saved others; himself he cannot save. If he be the King of Israel, let him now come down from the cross, and we will believe him. He trusted in God; let him deliver him now,

if he will have him: for he said, I am the Son of God."[1]

3. *The Word of Prayer*—uttered by the penitent malefactor, who in the midst of all that pain and ignominy was able to see a real royalty in his Fellow-Sufferer, and prays, "Lord, remember me when thou comest into thy kingdom."[2]

4. *The Word of Misunderstanding*—spoken by the Roman soldiers, when our Lord uttered that bitter cry, telling of His anguish and desolation, "Eli, Eli, lama sabachthani?" and the Roman soldiers, ignorant of the Hebrew language, caught at the first syllables and thought that as a superstitious Jew He was invoking Elijah: "This man calleth for Elias."[3]

5. *The Word of Acknowledgment* — called forth from the centurion, who watched by the Cross, and saw the moral majesty of this Sufferer, His patience and meekness, and saw, too, the awful portents which accompanied His death, when the sun hid his face, and the earthquake rent the rocks: "Truly this was the Son of God."[4] Indeed the claim He made was right and true. He was a supernatural person, God's representative.

We will meditate each day on one of these five sayings, and will try, with God's help, to think of what they meant as expressing the thoughts of those who stood round the Cross, and to hear their echo now in those who gaze on that wondrous mystery.

---

[1] S. Matt. xxvii. 42, 43.
[2] S. Luke xxiii. 42.
[3] S. Matt. xxvii. 47.
[4] S. Matt. xxvii. 54.

First, *the Word of Accusation*, the Title placed over His Head upon the Cross: "Jesus of Nazareth, the King of the Jews." It was customary that the charges against a criminal, the ground on which he was condemned, should be written out in brief on a tablet which was hung round his neck as he was led to execution. Pilate only followed out this plan. This was the charge the Jews and Chief Priests had brought before the Governor, when they dragged Jesus to the judgment-seat. He says, He is Messiah. At first they had spoken vaguely of His being "a malefactor," but Pilate demanded, What definite charge do you bring?[1] "We found him (they say) perverting the nation, and forbidding to give tribute to Cæsar, saying that he himself is Christ, a King."[2] Afterwards they mention the religious charge of blasphemy. "We have a law, and by our law he ought to die, because he made himself the Son of God."[3] And Pilate was the more afraid when he heard that claim; it fitted in with the dream of his wife, with the majesty and moral grandeur which he had already recognized in the Man before him; but officially he could take no notice of it. The civil charge is pressed. This was Pilate's business. "If thou let this man go, thou art not Cæsar's friend : whosoever maketh himself a king speaketh against Cæsar."[4] The Jews threatened to appeal to Cæsar, and that the Governor could not

---

[1] S. John xviii. 29.   [2] S. Luke xxiii. 2.
[3] S. John xix. 7.   [4] S. John xix. 12.

face. Pilate seeks favor with his imperial master, and he dare not incur suspicion of unfaithfulness to him. So he condemns Jesus to death as a rebel, a false king, though he knew that He was innocent. Then, partly in mockery and partly to have his revenge on the hated Jews and their leaders, he writes the accusation, "This is the King of the Jews." In mingled scorn and pity he had asked Jesus, "Art thou the King of the Jews?" This harmless, deserted man, this enthusiastic fanatic—a pretty king indeed! a fine rival to my imperial master! But the Jews have accused Him of claiming to be a king, and Pilate will show his contempt for their nation by calling this harmless enthusiast their king.

I. Think of *the injustice of the accusation.* Our Lord had repeatedly refused to be made a king.

After the miraculous feeding of the five thousand the people would have taken Him by force and made Him a king in the enthusiasm stirred by the miracle in the multitudes on their way to celebrate the Paschal feast.[1] They would have put Him at the head of that great caravan, and gone on to Jerusalem, prepared to fight for Him against the Roman usurper. He had sent away His disciples lest they too should be carried away by this desire of the multitude, and Himself had retired to the mountain-top to spend the night in prayer. It was the disappointment of the hopes the people had

---

[1] S. John vi. 15.

formed on Palm Sunday, when they welcomed Him to the city with Hosannas, as a king coming in the name of the Lord,[1] that had brought about the change to the shout of Good Friday, "Crucify Him!" They had thought, those Galilean peasants, that now with Him for their leader it would be an opportunity to make headway against the power of Rome, and when He failed to rise up to the dignity they would thrust upon Him, then they turned against Him.[2] He told them of His spiritual kingdom, but for such a kingdom they had no desire, and in their chagrin they left Him in the hands of His enemies, the Chief Priests, and allowed them to accuse Him of making a claim for not making which He had forfeited their allegiance.

How great the injustice with which He was treated! How bitter His pain and disappointment! And how true His sympathy with all who suffer like injustice! O suffering soul! misunderstood in thy family, maligned among friends, look to Jesus and learn like Him to commit thyself in calmness to Him that judgeth righteously.[3] Be content to be unknown, or mis-known—unknown to earth, if well known to Heaven. All that is intended for insult shall redound to thy true glory, even as it was with Him. He is executed on the public highway, that all may read the Title, and know Who it is

---

[1] S. Mark xi. 9, 10; S. Luke xx. 38.
[2] See this change of popular feeling wonderfully delineated in *Ben-Hur*, book viii., chapters v. and vi.
[3] 1 S. Pet. ii. 23.

that suffers, "The King of the Jews." So shall thy character be vindicated. Thy meekness and patience shall conform thee to thy Lord and make thee dear to Him. And in the day of His manifestation with His Saints thou shalt be found near Him.

Let us be prepared for the misunderstandings to which Christ's Church and religion may be exposed. Men would use them to help on some worldly scheme, or turn them to account for some political purpose; but shrink back from simple obedience to the law of life which He lays down, from following in His steps, saying, "We will not have this Man to reign over us."

Our Lord does indeed come to establish a kingdom far greater than that His enemies imagined. He came to instil principles that would render the tyranny of Rome harmless. He came to reign over hearts in love, a rule far grander than that of external force. A King He is, a King Whose service is perfect freedom; a King Who frees His subjects from the bondage of sin, the tyranny of Satan, the oppression of the World.

II. So consider further *the truth of the accusation*. The Chief Priests beg that the sentence may be altered. Write not, they say to Pilate, "The King of the Jews; but that he said, I am King of the Jews." But Pilate would not be dictated to. Insolently and tersely he replies, "What I have written I have written."[1] Not a word will I change. You asked

---

[1] S. John xix. 21, 22.

me to condemn Him as the King of the Jews, and so I have written. Another concerned in our Lord's condemnation had unconsciously prophesied, Caiaphas the High Priest, when he said it was expedient that one man should die for the people.[1] Pilate now likewise utters an unconscious prophecy when he inscribes the Title. He wrote truly, "This is the King of the Jews."

The Angel of the Annunciation had declared, "He shall be great, and shall be called the Son of the Highest: and the Lord God shall give unto him the throne of his father David."[2] Mary's Child was worshipped by Eastern sages as well as by the shepherds of Bethlehem. That tender Plant was indeed the Branch (the new Shoot—which is the meaning of "Nazarene") growing up in obscurity but destined to exercise a world-wide dominion;[3] before Whose throne at the last all nations shall be gathered to receive their final doom. Meanwhile He exercises a mighty sway over hearts which He draws unto Himself. "King of the Jews" He is, the heir of David's throne, but not only *their* King. He comes to establish His universal Church, in which all nations shall find their home, and each fulfil its own destiny. Of this Pilate unconsciously prophesied when he wrote the Title in three languages, that all might read it. It was written in Hebrew, that the people might under-

---

[1] S. John xi. 49–52; xviii. 14.   [2] S. Luke i. 32.
[3] S. Matt. ii. 23; Isa. xi. 1; liii. 2; Zech. iii. 8.

stand; in Latin, the language of the Roman court and of the soldiers; and in Greek, for the benefit of foreigners present for the Passover. It was intended for mockery, but it told of the universal character of Christ's kingdom. The City of God is built at the confluence of three streams — of Hebrew prophecy, of Greek literature and philosophy, of Roman organization and empire.

In Hebrew, Greek, and Latin is the Title written, that all nations may recognize their interest in the Crucified King. In Holy Week we pray to Mary's Child, the Seed of Abraham, that He would have mercy on His own favored people and on the Gentile nations who know Him not; that He would remove all blindness and hardness of heart, and that He would bring back to the way of truth all those who live in darkness and error; that He, our Shepherd King, would fetch all wanderers home to His flock, that they may be saved among His true Israelites.

III. Once more think of *the spiritual character of the King and of His Kingdom*. He was rejected by His subjects, not because He was unworthy of His kingdom but because they were unworthy of Him. Pilate acknowledged Him as a King, and we as we gaze upon the moral glory of His Passion recognize One Who is indeed King of men," Holiest among the mighty, mightiest among the holy." Yes, we bow before His Cross, because we recognize the Lord of glory there reigning on His throne. The moral glory, the grace and truth He there exhibits are such as indeed belong to the Only-begotten of the

Father.'¹ We pray Thee, blessed Jesu, to exercise Thy sovereign power over our hearts. To Thee we would bend our intellect, that in Thee we may attain true knowledge and wisdom ; to Thee we yield our affections, that from Thee we may learn true love ; to Thee we offer our will, that it may beat in harmony with Thine. Think of the supernatural character of the kingdom that the Crucified inaugurates. His throne, the Cross ; His sceptre, a reed ; His Crown, of thorns. He was teaching man the vanity of worldly wealth and honor ; that man's dignity consists in what he is, not in what he has ; that his greatness and worth is to be estimated not by the opinion of those round about, but by his own strength of character. Jesus showed Himself the true and perfect Man, to Whom the greatest and the lowest can do most loving homage. If we are to be subjects of His Kingdom we must learn its standards. Our nobility must be such as belongs to the inner man ; our treasure such as moth and rust cannot corrupt ; our glory not in worldly honor and human appreciation, but such as God, Who seeth in secret and trieth the heart, will bestow.

So let us meditate on the Title on the Cross, considering—

(1) The *injustice* of the accusation, and learn humbly and meekly to bear misunderstanding and misrepresentation :

(2) The *truth* unconsciously proclaimed in what

---

¹ S. John i. 14 ; 1 Cor. ii. 8.

Pilate wrote—How indeed He is the King, and we are to bring all the faculties of our nature to bow before Him, and by our prayers, our alms, and our influence to bring others to acknowledge His Kingdom :

(3) And ask that we may know the true standard and measures of His Kingdom, and so may judge with true and righteous judgment.

Psalm ii.

II.

THE WORD OF DERISION AND SCOFFING.

"He saved others; himself he cannot save. If he be the King of Israel, let him now come down from the cross, and we will believe him. He trusted in God; let him deliver him now, if he will have him: for he said, I am the Son of God."—S. MATTHEW xxvii. 39-43.

YESTERDAY we thought of the Title, the Accusation prepared by Pilate and affixed to the Cross. It marked out the charge for which sentence was passed upon Jesus, the charge of sedition, forbidding to give tribute to Cæsar, claiming Himself to be the King of the Jews. That was the only charge of which the Roman Governor could take cognisance, and sentence on it was extorted from him by the Chief Priests. Now we come to the second Saying addressed to our Lord upon the Cross. All these Sayings are representative Sayings, and all are spoken by representative persons; each expressing a different relation to our Lord. Pilate is the representative of Worldly Power, and speaks of Him as a usurping King, a feeble rival to his imperial master. He points in mockery to the Nazarene, "Behold the King of the Jews."

The taunt uttered by the Chief Priests is of a different character. "Come down from the Cross, and we will believe. He saved others: himself he cannot save. He trusted in God: let him deliver him now if he will have him; for he said, I am the Son of God." They mocked Him as a pretender to Messianic dignity. It was on the religious charge of blasphemy that they had determined to put Him to death. They trumped up the political charge to satisfy Pilate, but that was not the charge on which they had condemned Him in their own council. The High Priest said, I adjure thee by the living God, that thou tell us whether thou be the Christ, the Son of God. Jesus replied, Thou hast said. Hereafter shall ye see the Son of Man sitting on the right hand of power, and coming in the clouds of Heaven. Then the High Priest, pretending that his feelings were shocked and outraged, rent his clothes, and said, What need of further witnesses?[1] It was on the charge of blasphemy, for unwarranted religious claims that He was condemned, and for that they mock and jeer and jibe at Him hanging on the Cross. Mark, it was not the people but the Chief Priests that mocked. Those that passed by indeed wagged their heads and reviled Him; but they were put up to it by the Chief Priests. They had gone among the crowd at Pilate's judgment-seat and whispered to them to demand Barabbas instead of Jesus, and now others take up the cry they lead. We are to think of these taunts as they sounded in His ears, and as they expressed the mind of those who uttered them, and as they find their echo in all ages.

---

[1] S. Matt. xxvi. 63-66.

I. Think, then, of the *grief* of our Lord as He heard them, accentuated by the fact that the speakers were His own official representatives. The taunt would have been a comparatively little thing if said by the Roman soldiers or by Pilate, but from those whom He had placed in authority it was a most bitter pain to His tender Heart. "He came unto his own, and his own received him not."[1] He had foretold this detail of His Passion to His disciples as they went up to Jerusalem where He must suffer. "The Son of man shall be betrayed unto the chief priests and unto the scribes, and they shall condemn him to death, and shall deliver Him to the Gentiles to mock, and to scourge, and to crucify him."[2] Yes, His own representatives, who should have prepared the people to welcome Him by expounding the prophecies, and showing their fulfilment in Him, they stirred up the people to demand His death; they mocked Him!

When we receive no sympathy from those with whom we live, and with whom we would fain be at peace, or when those whose allies and instruments we would be fail to understand us, or when the purity of our motives is questioned—we suffer the like grief. The heart is sore just in proportion to its own generosity. And what was the pain and grief to Jesus when thus reviled by His own ministerial representatives! Think of His being charged with blasphemy against His Father. That was a far

---

[1] S. John i. 11.   S. Matt. xx. 18, 19.

deeper grief than the accusation of being a mock king. That would have been mere folly. Pilate thought of Him as a harmless enthusiast, a dreamer. But by the Chief Priests He is condemned on a charge of heresy. He, the Witness to the Truth, Who referred all He did to the Father, and said He came only to do His will [1]—that He should be accused of usurping unlawfully and illegitimately the position that belonged to Him! That He should be scorned as a Samaritan, as possessed by an evil spirit, He Who came to destroy the works of the Devil! [2]

And oh! the pain still greater to the Heart of Jesus to know that all the people were shaken in their belief in His innocence, when they saw that after these taunts He was left to die, shown (as they thought) to be rejected of God.

Ah! let us think of the grief of these revilings, remembering from whom they came, and we will take consolation when we are charged with disloyalty to the Church we love, to the principles we hold most dear. Indeed, Blessed Lord, there is no grief in which Thou canst not extend to us Thy sympathy.

II. Go on to consider *the taunt itself.* See how it really pointed to the manifestation of our Lord's glory. It was because their eyes were blinded, even though they held the position of religious teachers, that they recognized not His glory when hanging

---

[1] S. John v. 19, 30; vi. 38; xii. 49.
[2] S John viii. 48; 1 S. John iii. 8.

on the Cross. These secularized ecclesiastics were judging according to their own heart.

Blessed Lord, if Thou in justice hadst hearkened to that challenge, and come down from the Cross to manifest Thy power, our salvation would have been lost. When Thou didst save others, Thou wouldest not save Thyself. Thine enemies say, "Thou canst not;" and we say, "Thou wouldest not." It was by Thy self-sacrifice that Thou didst teach men a disinterested love. It was then Thou didst teach us true, generous love for others. Thou didst save us, because Thou wert willing to lay down Thine own life. By Thine obedience unto death Thou didst atone for man's disobedience, and thus didst rescue us. Thou didst show Thy Divine Sonship by not coming down from the Cross. An earthly Messiah would have sought to make some external manifestation of his power, but in Thy heroic fortitude and enduring patience Thou didst show a splendor of moral character far surpassing the worldly conception of those who mocked Thee.

Satan in the Wilderness approached our Lord with the like temptation. "If thou be the Son of God, command that these stones be made bread."[1] And because He was the Son of God He would accomplish the fast, waiting upon His Father; He would not satisfy the craving of the lower nature, and in the abstinence from any such gratification He would manifest His Divine Sonship.

---

[1] S. Matt. iv. 3.

Even so with the Church in every age: men mock and sneer at her poverty, her want of organization and earthly power; they ask, Can this be the Church of the living God—with all these divisions and anomalies, these spots and blots and stains? But God never promised on earth a Church without spot, or wrinkle, or any such thing. This is to be the glorious condition of the Church at the last. Here she is proved to be really the Bride of Christ by sharing His lot, for better and for worse.[1] She is shown to be His not by being endowed with great earthly gifts but by her likeness to her Lord. Founded on a Rock, but planted in the sea; upheld in life, though crucified in weakness, God delivers not His Church from suffering, so as to ward it off, but He delivers His people *out* of suffering, so that we are brought forth perfected thereby.

III. Think once more how *the taunt is continually repeated by us and to us.*

1. We so often think that if only we are trying to be on God's side we have a right to be exempted from crosses. At any rate from spiritual temptations, from dryness in prayer, from evil imaginations. Why so? Is not this the same sort of conception that led the Chief Priests to say, "If he be the Son of God, let God deliver him now, if he will have him." God's love does not exempt us, any more than it did Christ, from trials and sorrow. "Great are the troubles of the righteous: but the Lord delivereth

---

[1] Eph. v. 27; Rev. xix. 7, 8.

him out of all." [1] God does not exempt us now in a fallen world from trials. He shows His care in supporting us *in* trials. The shadow of the Cross we must expect to fall on those nearest and dearest to Him. Mary, His beloved Mother, stands by the Cross, the representative of the Church; and those who aspire to high places in His Kingdom are asked if they can drink of the cup of which He has drunk. I will not expect, then, in taking any fresh onward step to be exempt from trials. I will nerve myself to meet any sorrow, knowing that I shall be supported in it, that He will not suffer any temptation beyond my strength to try me. He Who has conquered *for* me will conquer *in* me.

2. And the same taunt we may think of as addressed *to* us by the worldly spirit calling us to come down from the Cross. It may be in the secular newspaper of the day, or by the voice of a friend: "Come down, show thyself to be the child of God by enjoying greater liberty. God's child surely will not be cramped in thought by the narrow limits of creeds, in life by rule, mortification, or restraint. Claim your portion of the good things of the world; enjoy life, allow free play to all the faculties of your nature." So speaks the worldly spirit. We reply, with Jesus: "Because I am God's Son, and have a higher life, therefore I am comparatively indifferent to merely worldly pleasure and honor. I am ready to sacrifice that which may be attractive,

---

[1] Ps. xxxiv. 19.

especially those things I know to be dangerous to my higher interests, lest I should lose my firm grasp on what is my true inheritance. Because I am God's child my heart is set on things above, and I am indifferent to the joys and sorrows that belong to this world. I am bent on so passing through things temporal that I lose not the things eternal. Because I am God's child I am prepared to follow along the Royal Road the Master has trodden before. I hear His voice, If thou wilt be My disciple, take up thy cross; that is the path that is marked by My footprints, that is the narrow way that leadeth to Life eternal.

Psalm lxix.

III.

THE WORD OF PRAYER.

"Lord, remember me when thou comest into thy Kingdom."—S. LUKE xxiii. 42.

WHAT a blessed contrast it is to turn from the Words addressed to our Lord on the Cross which we have already considered to the Word we have to consider now! We have thought of Pilate's mocking sentence, "This is the King of the Jews;" and of the words of taunt and sneer with which the Chief Priests and Rulers, secularized ecclesiastics, reviled our Lord as a false Messiah—"He trusted in God: let him deliver him now if he will have him." S. Matthew and S. Mark tell us that at the first the malefactors who were crucified with Him reviled Him also.[1] S. Luke, giving a fuller account, tells us that after a while one of the malefactors turned to our Lord with this prayer, and to that one we will now direct our thoughts.[2]

The malefactors had eagerly seized the stupefying draught which our Lord refused. He would not dull His consciousness in the struggle against sin, but would keep His powers to the very end. But they are eager to save themselves all the pain they can.

---

[1] S. Matt. xxvii. 44 ; S. Mark xv. 32.
[2] S. Luke xxiii. 39-43.

When the nails were driven into their hands they could hardly feel the pain from stupefaction; but after a while they, in half-consciousness—just as one coming out of ether hears half in dream and half in reality—catch snatches of what is said around the Cross, and they take up the jeers of the Chief Priests and "cast the same in His teeth."

We are not to think of them as being simple "thieves;" *robbers* is the right translation. They were wild, bold outlaws, such as infested the Galilean hills, and who with their robbery joined a rough patriotism, ready to rise up in revolt against the foreign power of Rome. They were members of such a band as that of which Barabbas had been chief, their hand against every man and every man's hand against them. Now they have come to execution and are going to brave it out to the last. But one of them, struck by such a sight as he had never seen before, is moved. He had seen, perhaps, our Lord in that imperturbable meekness before His accusers that had moved even Pilate.[1] He had heard Pilate declare that he found no fault in Him.[2] But the robbers had not then taken much account of Jesus, bent on learning their own fate. But this one had walked by our Lord's side on the road to Calvary, and had heard him speak to the daughters of Jerusalem, bidding them weep not for Him but for that which was coming upon the doomed city.[3]

---

[1] S. Mark xv. 2-5.   [2] S. John xix. 4.
[3] S. Luke xxiii. 27-32.

He had seen Jesus refuse the stupefying drug, and had heard His prayer for His murderers, and then he had become stupefied himself and heard no more. Now recovering consciousness, all he had seen before passes through his mind. He turns to gaze upon his fellow-sufferer and sees a wondrous moral majesty beaming from His face amid all the pain and humiliation. What manner of man is this? —he thinks—what if this *should* be the Messiah! His companion utters some special word of reviling, such as he before had joined in, and he turns to him, rebuking him. Dost not thou fear God, seeing thou art in the same condemnation? and we indeed justly; for we receive the due reward of our deeds: but this man hath done nothing amiss. Pilate said so, and since then he has done nothing! Then he turned to our Lord, with only a dim conception of Whom he was addressing. Perhaps some old teaching of the synagogue service comes before him, some scripture prophecy, such as Isaiah's description of the Messiah, as one who will come to heal the broken-hearted, to preach deliverance to the captives and the recovery of sight to the blind, to set at liberty them that are bruised.[1] Was not this the kind of work this Man had been doing? He had looked indeed for an earthly Messiah, but what matters now any earthly consideration? The idea of a spiritual deliverance comes before him, he has a vision of a spiritual kingdom. He prays, Lord,

---

[1] Isa. lxi. 1; S. Luke iv. 16–21.

remember me when Thou comest into Thy kingdom.

I. Think of the lesson of the contrast. The very publicans and harlots enter into the kingdom of God before the Chief Priests and Elders.[1] There is no blinding of the eyes here through envy. The Chief Priests had every tittle of evidence that this poor outlaw had. Pilate saw that they were blinded with envy. They steeled and hardened their hearts. There were moral obstacles to prevent their seeing the truth. They would not take the evidence of His miracles or listen to His words.[2] They had not the right dispositions. Consider the contrast between this poor robber and those who should have led the people. They had studied the prophecies, and yet they turn against Him, for the darkness of their own hearts cannot receive Him, while evidence far less than was offered to them convinces the poor outcast. So it is now. Some rich, favored nation, boastful of its civilization, really drawing its vitality from the Christianity with which it is surrounded, rejects Christ's truths, while some poor, down-trodden race, acknowledging its own inability to rise up to higher things, eagerly accepts Him. He ever comes, not to call the righteous but sinners to repentance. On the Cross, as always, it is the rich He sends empty away, but the hungry He fills with good things.[3] On the Cross He is seen as the good

---

[1] S. Matt. xxi. 31.   [2] S. John v. 36–47; viii. 47.
[3] S. Matt. ix. 12, 13; S. Luke i. 53.

physician healing the sick, while they that are whole have no need of the physician. O blessed Jesu, break down within us all pride and envy, all unwillingness to acknowledge ourselves mistaken, to submit to Thy holy will; do away in us with all moral obstacles that bind and blind, that so we may be prepared to acknowledge Thy truth.

II. And then think, too, how this Word sounded in the ears of our blessed Lord. What a refreshment amid the taunts of His enemies to hear this prayer—the faith dim, but the prayer very earnest and sincere—" Lord, remember me." He is making an act of faith according to his opportunities, making the best prayer he can. Our Lord is refreshed and consoled. He begins to see of the travail of His soul, and is satisfied.[1] The words come like drops of water to the parched earth. Now, lifted up, He begins to draw all men unto Him.[2] His sweet forbearance conquers. He triumphs in the midst of suffering. Love conquers all. God had tried, if we may so say, by the terrors of the Law to subdue man, and the Law had failed. He places Himself in the midst of fallen humanity in a condition of suffering to draw out man's pity, and so He wins his love. Think of the consolation of Jesus, and think of this as marking out the law of all Christian conquest, by meekness and self-sacrifice, by forbearance rather than by rigorous reproach, for any who will win souls to truth and virtue, to Christ and God.

---

[1] Isa. liii. 11. [2] S. John xii. 32.

Only in His way can we, can the Church, hope to reproduce His victory.

Ah, blessed Jesu! this is the law of Thy conquest. The Cross conquers, because the Cross is the well of love. We pray that lifted up afresh in Passiontide Thou wilt touch hearts with Thy love. Kindle our souls with true devotion; renew the devotion we have felt in past years, only let there be true devotion and less of mere feeling; give us the earnest desire to do and bear for Thee, Who hast done and borne so much for us. And bless, we pray Thee, all preaching of the Cross in foreign lands, and by those who tell of Thy love to the heathen. Speak through their lips and draw all to Thyself. Draw the unbelievers, the impenitent, the backsliders, draw us all, that we may in truth "run after Thee."[1]

III. Think of the prayer as expressing the mind of him who uttered it. The prayer of a sufferer, purified, softened by suffering, addressed to a suffering Lord. It is when life is ebbing out, when earthly visions are fading away, that this poor robber is led to higher things. God has shown him the vanity of all else. Suffering is intended to be remedial. God in His compassion will accept even the dregs of a life, that He may renew that life. Suffering is intended to purify the vision, that as the outward man decays we may be led to set our affections on those things which cannot pass away.

---

[1] Cant. i. 4; Ps. cxix. 82.

O blessed Jesu, we pray Thee to hallow suffering to all Thy people. Grant that they may not be hardened, but teach them to accept suffering with right dispositions, that their hearts may be touched, their lives sanctified. Hallow all bereavement, all spiritual trials and sorrows. In Passiontide we beg Thee to win souls to Thee through Thy suffering.

Suffering is a kind of sacrament, requiring right dispositions in those who receive it. In those two crucified beside our Lord we see the different effects of suffering: one is hardened, the other is softened; one reviles our Lord to the end, the other turns to Him in penitence and prayer.[1] Grant me, dear Lord, rightly to accept suffering, and then send what Thou wilt. Only purify me, and grant that, dying with Thee, I may attain to live with Thee.

The Word we are considering was the prayer of a sufferer, and addressed to a suffering Lord, the prayer the suffering Lord led him to offer. He saw our Lord sharing his suffering, and so felt sure that He could sympathize with him. Ah, blessed Lord, it is because I can pray to Thee, "by Thy Fasting, by Thy Temptation, by Thine Agony and Bloody Sweat, by Thy Cross and Passion, by Thy Death and Burial," that I feel sure Thou canst understand me. This is one of the greatest blessings which the Incarnation assures to me. I think of God in His own

---

[1] Comp. Rev. ix. 20, 21; xvi. 8–11.

Divine Nature, and I feel a doubt if He, though my Heavenly Father, can understand my pain, my temptations and falls. But the Incarnate Lord has been tempted in all points like as we are, can in all points sympathize with and succor those that are tempted.[1]

In visiting the sick and poor remember how the uneducated and ignorant rejoice to hear the story of the Lord's sufferings. Often the eye, almost glazed in death, is turned to the figure of the Lord upon the Cross, and the sufferer is nerved to endure to the very end, knowing that the Lord Himself has gone the same way before. We are nerved to bear the parting with relatives, as we think of His parting with His blessed Mother; nerved to bear spiritual desolation, as we think of His bitter cry of anguish, and remember the clouding of His Soul; enabled to commend our soul to God as we re-echo His last words, "Into Thy hands I commend My Spirit."

So we would take the prayer addressed to our Lord on the Cross as the prayer in which we would speak to Him now, and beg that, with confession of our sin, in true faith and hope in Him, we may be enabled at our last hour to say, Lord, remember me in Thy kingdom: Thy kingdom is set up upon the Cross: Thou art the King of Paradise.

May I, persevering to the end, in any temptation or sorrow, in bearing the consequences of past

---

[1] Heb. ii. 18 ; iv. 15.

sin, suffer with Thee here, O Lord, that so I may reign with Thee hereafter. May my last hour be hallowed by union with Thee, and so may I be welcomed into Thy kingdom, which by Thy Cross and precious Blood Thou didst win for us.

Psalm. cxxx.

IV.

THE WORD OF MISUNDERSTANDING.

"Behold, he calleth Elias. Let us see whether Elias will come to take him down."—S. MARK xv. 35, 36.

How wonderfully lifelike is the scene of the Crucifixion as depicted by the several Evangelists! How true to his natural position does each one appear whose actions are recorded!

Pontius Pilate, as the Roman Governor, takes cognizance of the political charge, and affixes the title to the cross, "The King of the Jews." The Chief Priests, as they had charged Jesus with religious blasphemy, taunt and mock Him as a pretended Messiah. The penitent robber, brought up as a child to attend the Synagogue and Temple services, had mingled with his outlawry and robbery dreams of patriotism. His mind is purified by suffering, and as earthly visions fade away he beholds a real royalty in his Fellow-Sufferer, and the teaching of the Old Testament Scriptures, long buried in his heart and mind, flashes up; he feels, Here is One indeed on whom the Spirit rests, One who has come to heal the broken-hearted, to preach good tidings to the meek, to proclaim liberty to the captives, and the restoring of sight to the blind; he sees fulfilled the old description, he recognizes God's Messiah, the spiritual King reigning on the Cross, and he prays, "Lord, remember me when Thou comest into Thy kingdom."

The Roman soldiers, too, act in perfect accordance with their position and circumstances. They are there simply on duty. They are ordered to watch by the Cross until the end. They have no interest in the matter, and, brutalized by their familiarity with such scenes, they have their dice to wile away the time while waiting, and the sour wine they have brought for their refreshment. They could not be expected to understand spiritual things, and so when our Lord cries out, in the words of the twenty-second Psalm, "Eli, Eli, lama sabachthani?" (the very language is strange to them, they only know a few detached words of the despised Hebrew language), they not unnaturally, knowing that the Jews expected Elijah to intervene on their behalf in any crisis, that it was supposed to be his office to conduct souls to Paradise, think that the sufferer is invoking the Prophet. The next cry followed immediately on this, "I thirst," and a soldier, moved with pity, dips a sponge in the wine, and on a reed of hyssop puts it to His lips. The others say, Let alone, don't get in the way, let us see if Elias will come to help him.[1] The whole scene is just what we might have expected; the soldiers were utterly unable to realize the meaning of

---

[1] S. Matt. xxvii. 46–49; S. Mark, xv. 34–36; S. John, xix. 28, 29.

that cry to God; they suppose that in His agony Jesus calls for Elijah.

I. Think of the pain with which those words rise up in His ears, as those for whom He dies show their inability to understand Him. It had been so all through His life. "They daily mistake my words."[1] The Jews sought to entrap him.[2] His very disciples were so slow to take in His teaching.[3] Up to the very last, while He sought to teach the great lesson of the self-abandonment of love, they were quarrelling about pre-eminence.[4] And now, in His last dying moments, those for whom He was laying down His life misunderstand Him. It is the sorrow of one far beyond his age, who towers above his fellows, the sorrow of being thus misunderstood. Think of the loneliness of Jesus on the Cross—external and internal. He is betrayed by one disciple, denied by another, forsaken by all. True, there is a little group near the Cross—Mary, His beloved Mother, and John, who, immediately recovering himself, had followed on to the High Priest's palace, to Pilate's judgment hall, to Calvary, and as a reward of his faithfulness had received that precious gift, the only earthly gift He has to bestow, the care of His blessed Mother. And Mary Magdalene is there with others, obliged to stand at a distance, driven off by the ribald jests and rude thrusts of the sol-

---

[1] Ps. lvi. 5.   [2] S. Matt. xxii. 15.
[3] S. Luke xxii. 38; S. Matt. xv. 16; S. John xiv. 9.
[4] S. Luke xxii. 24.

diers. The Chief Priests have been reviling Him, but are now departed to the evening service in the Temple, gone off to offer their empty rites with blood-stained hands, having turned their backs on the true Paschal Lamb offered for the sins of the world. The soldiers only are left, and they are only waiting for all to be over. Think of the loneliness external and internal.

O blessed Jesu, we would now take our place in the company of the faithful few; open our eyes that we may see, touch our hearts that we may weep with Mary Magdalene, and enable us, like Thy dear Mother, to stand bravely by Thy Cross. John saw Thee with the eye of faith, that could behold the things of God, saw Thee reign on the tree of shame in moral majesty and begin to draw all men to Thyself. Grant us too so to gaze in the sacred hours of Thy Passion; give to us the seeing eye, the listening, understanding heart.

II. Think of the soldiers' Word of Misunderstanding, how it is ever re-echoed through the ages. Jesus spake not simply to those within ear-shot, but to every age and every nation. We may be sure that the words addressed to Him that are set down in the Gospels are representative words; and as the Word of Taunt and Scoffing we hear continually repeated, and pray that the sufferer's Prayer to a suffering Lord may be continually on our lips, so this too must be a representative word. The World has no real power of apprehending spiritual things. Spiritual things are spiritually discerned.[1] The World must misunderstand, it has not the eye to see, or the ear to hear, or the scales to measure the things of God. Spiritual wisdom is foolishness to the natural man. It is as if one who was color-blind should take upon himself to judge of some great painting, or one without ear for music should criticise the harmony of some intricate composition; even so the natural heart of man is utterly incapable of judging of the things of God. Yet the World continually tries to do so. We presume to weigh all things in the finite scales of our puny understanding. We lay down what God ought to do; we determine what must be the lot of men in a future world, from what seems to us more likely; or we denounce the system of sacraments of grace because it is not such as we should have devised. We are just like the soldiers who had not the spiritual faculties to comprehend. Alas! how often we allow ourselves to be disturbed by the World's want of appreciation. The World scoffs at asceticism, at high ideas of prayer, and calls men of prayer mere dreamers and fanatics—and we think such things must be folly because the World in its wisdom derides them. The World in its wisdom knew not God.[2] There is a common-sense of faith which is clear to the illuminated heart. There are spiritual truths equally certain with those of nature, only requiring spiritual discernment; and shall we be disturbed because an article in a newspaper, written perhaps by some

---

[1] 1 Cor. ii. 14.   [2] 1 Cor. i. 21.

one of an indifferent, if not openly immoral life, fails to grasp the deep meaning of spiritual things? Because the libertine says, All will come right in the end, are we going to believe him instead of the teaching of the Church and Holy Scripture? What the World may say about religion we may be pretty sure is a perversion and caricature. Of this we may be quite sure, it is not the truth of God in its purity. We will not be guided in spiritual things by merely worldly reasoning. We will ask the way of true peace and holiness from those who have trodden in its paths. We will ask concerning the things of God from those who are His intimate and familiar friends. The World must misunderstand and misrepresent. From the World's ways and the World's opinions I appeal to the example of Thy Saints, O Lord, whom Thou hast filled with Thy gifts of light and truth and purity.

III. Let me think how incomprehensible that cry of Jesus must have been to the soldiers. It was not a cry of despair, though of mighty anguish and intense suffering, a cry from Christ as Man and as a Son to God His Father. Alone, deserted by His friends, turned from by those who should have been His willing servants, amid enemies, like "the hind at bay," [1] our Lord seems for the time to have lost the consciousness of the Divine love. The darkness of the earthly scene is a type of the deeper darkness of that clouded human Soul bereft of the conscious-

---

[1] See the title of Ps. xxii.

ness of the Divine favor. After a while the darkness passes away, and He cries, in the words of the Psalm, "My God, my God, why *didst* Thou forsake Me?" It is no complaint but the confident remonstrance of one whose trust is unshaken. The beginning of the Psalm is indeed a deep wail; it ends with triumphant expression of victory.

Yes, that cry told of two things that the World must ever misrepresent.

1. It told of the thirst of the soul for God. All others might have forsaken Me, but why didst Thou forsake Me? Betrayed by Judas, denied by Peter, mocked by the Chief Priests, smitten by the soldiers, I seem ensnared like a hind at bay. But this I could have borne, "Alone, yet not alone, because the Father is with Me." But oh, now when the light of Thy countenance is hid from me—"My soul is athirst for God, yea even for the living God." "Like as the hart desireth the water-brooks, so longeth my soul after thee, O God."[1] The World cannot understand this. The World thinks such expressions of devotion tell of an unhealthy, morbid sentimentality. "Don't indulge such thoughts and ideas," the World says. "Do your duty and then you will come to God, if there is one, in due time—but fellowship with God now is only mysticism." The World thinks of any soul seeking the Religious Life, it can only be turning to God because the World has failed; she has been crossed perhaps in love,

---

[1] Ps. xlii. 1, 2.

and, weary and disappointed, is just calling for some Elias.

2. That cry told of our Lord's thirst for God, and of the depth of penitence as He groaned under the burden of sin upon the Cross, felt the burden as He alone could feel it. The World does not understand penitence. The World thinks it is morbid to practise self-examination. It says: "Forget the past—as if God remembered, or cared to have you remember." David says, "My sin is ever before me,"[1] but that only shows a diseased state of mind. The World cannot understand contrition, which is the form love must take when sin has come in between the soul and God. But with John and the blessed Mother, and those who catch His Mind and reproduce His Spirit, let us stand before the Cross and gaze. We would seek, O blessed Jesu, to comprehend the meaning of what Thou doest, what Thou sayest and bearest. We would seek to follow in Thy footsteps; we acknowledge Thy moral glory on the tree of shame, and we would humble ourselves in penitence, and seek to rise up to that love, the perfect example of which Thou dost give to us.

Psalm xxii.

---

[1] Ps. li. 3.

V.

THE WORD OF ACKNOWLEDGMENT.

"Truly this was the Son of God."—S. MATTHEW xxvii. 54.

WE come to the consideration of the last words spoken to or concerning our Lord upon the Cross. The Words spoken to Him or those spoken by Him on the Cross have an undying significance. They are representative Words, expressing the different attitude to our Lord of those who uttered them. And the last Word spoken of Him on the Cross has a close correspondence with the last Word spoken by Him from the Cross. Both tell of the vindication of His glory. As the cloud rolled away which had clouded His consciousness of the Father's love, there was the pleading of His Divine Sonship, and in His last Word He claimed that Sonship in full confidence.

I. Spoken to Him or of Him there had been the sentence of Pilate, the taunt of the Chief Priests, the prayer of the malefactor, the misunderstanding of the soldiers, and now there is the confession of the centurion. It is recorded by the first three Evangelists. S. Mark tells us the centurion "stood over against" the Cross.[1] He as the officer was naturally a man of more intelligence and education than the

---

[1] S. Mark xv. 39.

common soldiers. They had formed a little knot by themselves, and were distributing the garments. The officer stands on one side from them, and draws near to the Cross. While they were intent on their dice he watched more curiously and intently. He caught the words spoken by our Lord. S. Mark tells us that it was the loud cry with which our Lord resigned His Spirit into the Father's hands that called forth the centurion's acknowledgment.[1] He had been impressed and awed by the preternatural darkness, when the midday sun veiled his face at this awful tragedy—as the midnight heavens had blazed with glory when the Angels announced the Saviour's Birth.

And he felt the earthquake that rent the rocks and opened the graves.[2] He heard the loud, victorious shout, telling of the accomplishment of His work, "It is finished!" The prize is won, the victory gained![3] And he thought, Never dying man spake like this. He had seen His meekness and patience and forbearance, His moral majesty, all through those dying hours. He had heard Him pray for His murderers; had heard the prayer of the dying robber, and He, the dying man, had promised His fellow-sufferer a place in His kingdom. What did all this mean? *Who* could this be making such claims in the face of death? An impostor would have been cowed then, a fanatic would have broken down.

---

[1] S. Mark xv. 39; comp. S. Luke xxiii. 47.
[2] S. Matt. xxvii. 54.   [3] S. John xix. 30.

Truly there is something in this man's claims. The centurion could not understand as we do His real relation to the Godhead, God of God, very God of very God, the only begotten Son of the Father—but he had heard the Chief Priests taunt this sufferer with claiming to be God's Son, and the centurion recognizes that He is "a righteous man,"[1] moreover that He had a Divine Mission. In some sense He claimed to be God's Son, and in that sense in which He made the claim, "truly this was the Son of God."[2] All His claims were true, He is indeed recognized as being what He claimed to be.

Ah, blessed Jesu, Thou didst gain the centurion's faith ; gain our faith. We believe in Thee, we worship Thee, because Thou didst not, wouldst not, come down from the Cross to manifest Thy Divine Sonship. They knew not Whom they crucified, even the Lord of glory.[3] We believe that Thou art the Son of God. How must we worship Thee, knowing Who Thou art. That Body was the Body of the Eternal Son of God made Man, that Soul was the Soul of God, having no existence apart from the

---

[1] S. Luke xxiii. 47.

[2] There is no definite article in the Greek of either S. Matt. xxvii. 54 or S. Mark xv. 39. "God's Son," as in the margin of the Revised Version, would best express the undefined sense of the centurion's words. The sense in which our Lord had made the claim, as equivalent to that of the Nicene Creed, is clear from many passages, *e.g.*, S. Matt. xxvi. 63-65 ; S. John xix. 7-9; v. 17-26; x. 30-33.

[3] 1 Cor. ii. 8.

THE WORD OF ACKNOWLEDGMENT. 49

Eternal Person Who in Mary's womb assumed our nature by the operation of the Holy Ghost. "Lift up your heads, eternal gates," the Angels sing. "Who is the King of glory?" the warders of the nether world in wonder reply, "The Lord" Who has proved Himself "mighty in battle," tried, assaulted, but victorious through all.[1] We worship Thee, O blessed Jesu, dead upon the Cross; we worship Thy living Person, who didst give Thy life for us, Who dost give Thyself to us in the Blessed Sacrament of the Altar, where Thou dost communicate to us the virtue of Thy saving Death, the merits of Thy Passion, a principle of undying Life. Think of the acknowledgment of the centurion, and think how it was won, by patience, and by the display of moral majesty in the midst of external pain and shame. Even so, if we would gain a victory over others, it is not by self-assertion, but by self-sacrifice that we are to conquer. Jesus reigns on the tree. Through death He wins life.

II. Consider God's vindication of His Son. "Verily thou art a God that hidest thyself."[2] The Word tabernacled in our flesh, that we might not be overcome by His glory. And God allowed His Son to be cast out of His vineyard, and slain by evil men.[3] But a day shall come when the righteous judgment of God shall vindicate itself.[4] On the third day He shall be "declared to be the Son

---

[1] Ps. xxiv. [2] Isa. xlv. 15. [3] S. Luke xx. 13-15.
[4] Rom. ii. 5; Acts iv. 10; v. 30, 31.

of God with power by the resurrection from the dead."[1] But no sooner is the obedience perfected than the reward begins. No sooner has Jesus spoken the last Word of Commendation to His Father than the Word of Acknowledgment is spoken of Him. No sooner has He humbled Himself even to the death of the Cross than God begins to exalt Him. Unto Him every knee shall bow, and every tongue confess that Jesus Christ is Lord.[2] The centurion's acknowledgment is the pledge of the fulfilment of the promise. Now at eventide it is light. We need not wait till the dawn for God's mercies to be shown. So quickly the return is given, so soon the reward bestowed.

O blessed Jesu, in Thy example of faithful obedience unto death, in Thy true love, Thy victorious self-sacrifice, let me learn the pattern for my own life. Let the mind be in me that was in Thee, and then shall be true of me the promise, that he that humbleth himself shall be exalted.[3]

III. Thus are we too to look for vindication to the end of the strife, when the battle is accomplished and the victory won. Using now the grace the Head bestows upon His members, at the last He shall be manifested with all His Saints. Then shall the Righteous Man, and all who have shared His righteousness, stand before His foes, and they shall say:

---

[1] Rom. i. 4 ; S. Luke xviii. 33.
[2] Phil. ii. 8-11 ; Rom. xiv. 10, 11.
[3] S. Luke xiv. 11.

"This is he, whom we had sometimes in derision ; we fools counted his life madness, and his end to be without honor : How is he numbered among the children of God, and his lot is among the saints!"[1]

But then the vindication is to be earned by us according to the same law. The World says to us "Come down ;" we will accept the Church if it manifest earthly power, and the Christian if his life is full of a large liberty. The World did not accept Jesus on the Cross, and the World will not accept His mystical Body on the Cross, or the individual Christian. And yet while crucified in weakness, Jesus reigns in power, in His own person and in His members.[2] We are to prove our Divine sonship, not by turning stones into bread or by throwing off restraints, but by living on whatever shall be the word of God for us, by being able to do without whatever may seem most necessary in life if He withhold it, by being able to cling to the Cross through all trial : so shall we be able to live in spotless integrity, and commend our spirits, made in His image, into His hands at the last, proved to be His children by our likeness to Himself. Stripped, if it be His will, of all, like the dead Body of Christ upon the Cross, deserted by friends, despoiled of goods, bereft of honor, our cherished wishes, plans, hopes frustrated : so surely shall we imitate His example, so shall Divine virtue be recognized in us, which, assaulted and tried, yet persevered through all

---

[1] Wisd. v. 1–5.   [2] 2 Cor. xiii. 4.

these temptations. So will we look forward to the manifestation of God's judgment when we have been proved and perfected by suffering. God divides His righteous Servant a portion with the great, and He divides the spoil with the strong ; because He poured out His Soul unto death ; and He was numbered with the transgressors ; and He bare the sin of many, and made intercession for the transgressors. So He makes His grave with the powerful, and is with the rich in His death ; because He had done no violence, neither was any deceit in His mouth.[1]

O blessed Jesu, our Lord and Master, Thee we worship, in Thee we believe, in Thee we hope, and Thee we would love more truly. Draw us that we may run after Thee, strengthen us to imitate Thy example, that so we may be acknowledged by Thee at the last.

> "Soul of Jesus, make me pure,
> Flesh of Jesus, be my cure,
> Fill me, O most precious Blood,
> Wash me, O thou mingled Flood ;
> Let Thy Passion banish fear,
> And my prayer, good Jesu, hear."

Psalm iv.

---

[1] Isa. liii. 9, 12.

GOOD FRIDAY MEDITATIONS.

The Words Spoken by our Lord from the Cross.

I.

THE TRUE REGARD OF SINNERS.

" Father, forgive them; for they know not what they do."
—S. LUKE xxiii. 34.

1. THE First Word tells of God's *regard of Sinners*, the regard of pity, infinite pity. His attitude toward them, yearning over them, is represented by Christ with His arms stretched out upon the Cross. This, you say, was by violence. Aye, and here is the glory, the wondrous culminating point of the manifestation of Divine love. Man rejects God. God bears with him, His sinful creature. He destroys him not. He suffers His attributes to be outraged. As they blindfolded Christ; God does not see, man says. They mocked Him; He can't interfere, they think, He is tied by laws; or He doesn't much care. His power is defied, His wisdom denied, His love outraged.

Death and Life meet in wondrous strife, Heaven and Hell, Love and Hate. The victory in the end remains with Love. God is not overcome of evil: He overcomes evil with goodness.

In Creation God loaded man with benefits. In Redemption, by a still greater manifestation of His goodness He would restore him. He seeks to win man back. He dispels the hard thoughts man has entertained of Him.

In Christ on the Cross praying for those who murdered Him we have the revelation of God's pitying love for sinners. He makes excuse for them: "They know not what they do." The chief priests, Judas, knew not *what* they did. Had they known he was the Lord of Glory they would not have crucified Him.[1] The soldiers were but executing their professional duty. All is wrong, unjust, cowardly, brutal, treacherous. Pride, envy, covetousness are at the bottom of it all. But still He makes all possible allowance. He seeks to draw sinners out of their sin, to show the real evil of the sins which partly in ignorance they commit. So He deals with us. We knew not what we did. More and more, year after year, we *do* know the real character of our sins. But in that surrender to lust, in that unbelief or disobedience, we realized not *what* we were doing—the offence against God, His interest in the matter.

2. As God's regard of sinners, so the true Man's we see in Jesus. It is illustrated in the touching story told by S. John of our Lord's dealing with

---

[1] 1 Cor. ii. 8; Acts iii. 17.

the woman taken in adultery. "Neither do I condemn thee: go, and sin no more," is the word of Jesus.[1] Before Him, the pattern of perfect purity, the sinner is abashed. See the true priestly spirit, not of harsh condemnation, but of yearning compassion. Do we cherish this spirit in dealing with "unfortunates," in thinking of "the criminal classes?" Do we take into account, and make allowance for, their disadvantages, the influence of heredity and environment? There is a danger in our "scientific philanthropy" of our becoming hard. Pure science is very cruel and unfeeling. It talks of the survival of the fittest; it may even go so far as to recommend us to let the depraved and apparently hopeless die off, while we concern ourselves only with the education of the children, with preventive rather than with remedial work. Christian love must mitigate the hard laws of social economy. "Father, forgive them; for they know not what they do."

Remember, too, the lesson with regard to those who offend *us*. It is easy to take a light view of sin in the abstract; it is very different when it touches us.

But in the true man hatred for sin must always be accompanied by love and pity for the sinner.

>Ps. cxxx.
>Collect, 3d for Good Friday.
>Hymn, "Sweet the moments."

[1] S. John viii. 11.

II.

OF PENITENTS.

"Verily I say unto thee, To-day shalt thou be with me in paradise."—S. LUKE xxiii. 43.

THE Second Word from the Cross shows us Christ our Lord, both God and Man, in His treatment of *Penitents*. In the First Word we see Him pitying, praying for, seeking to convert Sinners; in the Second He reconciles the Penitent.

1. *He has won a Sinner*. The triumphs of the Cross begin right soon. The lawless malefactor, a hardened criminal, the member of a band of brigands, of which very likely Barabbas was chieftain, at last after many hairbreadth escapes has been apprehended; caught perhaps red-handed, having shared in the murder which accompanied the insurrection.[1] He has been condemned to execution, and in order to add indignity to our Lord's crucifixion the rebels are to be put to death all together. Truly our Lord is "numbered with the transgressors." And He seizes the opportunity. Placing Himself in the midst of those whom He would help He gains access to them. He gives to us the example of sympathetic help—not preaching down to

---

[1] S. Mark xv. 7; S. Luke xxiii. 19.

others from a pedestal as "*You* sinners," but placing ourselves by their side that we may say "*We* sinners," and help them to rise.

Are we forward to use such opportunities, like S. Paul in prison laying himself out to win Onesimus,[1] or S. Vincent de Paul condemned to the galleys converting his fellow-prisoners?

The robber has never before been treated with kindness. He had been an outcast, who had forfeited all consideration. And treated hardly he has grown more hard himself; his hand against every man and every man's hand against him. But something good there was in him. And this display of meekness in Jesus appeals to it, and draws it out. He has watched Jesus in the Judgment Hall, on the Way of Sorrows, and on the Cross by his side. He is won by His unearthly majesty, His unconquerable patience.

> "The hardness and the stains of many a year
> Dropt off as in a moment and disclosed
> The nobler features of the new-born man." [2]

He turns to the Sufferer by his side and prays, "Lord, remember me when thou comest into Thy kingdom."

2. *And Jesus welcomes the Penitent.* There is nothing much that he can show in the way of peni-

---

[1] Philem. 9, 10.
[2] See Dean Plumptre's remarkable poem, "Jesus Bar-abbas," in his volume, *Lazarus and other Poems*.

tence. A deed of repentance he indeed shows in his rebuke to his companion, "Dost not thou fear God, seeing we are in the same condemnation? and we indeed justly, for we receive the due reward of our deeds." A full confession he cannot make; but, as Bishop Jeremy Taylor says, commenting on the great commission to remit and to retain sins, the Priest is a judge rather of the person's *penitence* than of his sins. The commission runs, "*Whose soever* sins," not *Whatsoever* sins.[1] And his faith is very imperfect. He acknowledges the Sufferer by his side as the Messiah, but he knows little either of His real dignity or of the true character of His kingdom. But Jesus does not insist on impossible —practically impossible—conditions. He will not break the bruised reed, nor quench the smoking flax. The man does what he can. Our Lord makes the very most of all. And so He would have us act. Don't make it too hard for people to return. How do we treat penitents in the House of Mercy, or the Temperance Society, or persons with sceptical doubts? Do we try to meet them halfway and help them to rise to higher, better things. Or do we hold our skirts and treat them as pariahs? So we are little likely to rescue them from their evil condition. Sin is horrid, loathsome; but out of the sin we must seek with infinite patience and tenderness to save the sinner.

---

[1] S. John xx. 23. See Jeremy Taylor, *Dissuasive from Popery*, Second Part, bk I., sect. xi. 2.

OF PENITENTS.   59

Listen to the Lord's reply: "To-day shalt thou be with Me in Paradise." He accepts the penitent so graciously : He promises more than was asked.

> "When the answer came it spake
> Of no proud pageant of the pomps of earth,
> But gave the promise of a night of peace
> After that noon of torture; cooling streams
> After that fevered thirst ; for writhing limbs
> And naked shame, and taunts of mocking crowds
> The land as Eden fair, where gales of balm
> O'er soft, green meadows murmur evermore.
> Fear not ; thou shalt be with Me ; so the words
> Like low, soft music sounded in his ears,
> With Me, within the Paradise of God."

3. Much still remains to be done. The sinner is won. The penitent is reconciled. There is need of subsequent training. In Paradise he shall learn lessons he did not learn, there was no one to teach him, here. He shall be more and more cleansed from the stain of sin. He shall be taught to see the truth, and in the light of that truth to see the old life. In perfected penitence shall be perfected purification.

Ps. xxxii.
Collect, Ash Wednesday.
Hymn, "All ye who seek for sure relief."

III.

OF FRIENDS.

"Behold thy son! Behold thy mother!"—S. JOHN xix. 26, 27.

WE have seen our Lord's conduct toward, His view of, *Sinners*, as He prayed for those who crucified Him, and of *Penitents*, as He pardons the malefactor. Now we see Him dealing with His *Friends*, His Mother and S. John.

1. He looks around. What does He see and hear?

The malefactors have relapsed into silence; the one stupefied and his strength spent, the other pondering. What were the operations of grace in his soul in that hour! The soldiers are playing dice to while away the time. Every now and then they join in with the Chief Priests as they hear some outrageous scoff. "I say! Do you hear that? Let's toast the King; come, drink his health." The Chief Priests are exulting in the execution of their plan. They wag their heads, and mock, deride, and taunt Him. The people join in the jeers.

Are there no friendly faces? He sees His Mother, tearful but brave, her heart broken, but she faints not nor shrieks. She stands by the Cross in a majesty of sorrow. Magdalene is in a paroxysm of grief, the other women are trying to quiet her. And He sees the disciple whom He loved. Aye, S. John is there.

Peter had slunk away; afraid at first, and now ashamed. All had been, as He foretold, offended, because of Him. Those whom He had called friends, not servants, they had left Him in the hands of His enemies. S. John had tripped, but he had soon recovered himself. And then he followed right on— *into* the High Priest's palace, to the Roman governor's prætorium. To him we owe the detailed account of the examination of our Lord before Pilate.[1] He had conducted the blessed Mother to Calvary. His love was strong even to death. He returned love for love. He is the loved disciple and the loving. He followed from the Breaking of Bread to the Drinking of the Cup of the Passion; from the Upper Chamber of the Eucharist to Gethsemane and Gabbatha and Golgotha.

2. And Jesus recognizes him standing by the Cross. Did He look for others? He recognizes him. In that recognition we have an illustration of "the living God" acting toward us as we act toward Him; really grieved by our unfaithfulness, really pleased by our fidelity. It is not an abstract law that we obey, but a living, loving, personal God and Master. He *sees* all, but He *looks* for that which He can reward. A cup of cold water given in His Name shall not be without its reward.[2] No work of mercy, corporal or spiritual, no self-denial, or resistance to temptation, shall be left unnoticed. He watches, He notes, aye, and He will reward openly.

---

[1] S. John xviii., xix.   [2] S. Matt. x. 42.

John is rewarded for his faithfulness. Jesus commends to his care His blessed Mother. What a reward for faithfulness! What honor and joy! "The Teacher who had been to him as a brother leaves to him a brother's duty. He is to be as a son to the Mother who is left desolate."

3. Note the nature of the reward. He is allowed to do something for Jesus. He is called to show love in a new way. Do not think that the reward for faithfulness will be discharge from further service. It will rather be increased responsibility, wider influence, a more serious charge. Favors involve duties; privileges bring with them responsibilities. Show love, our Lord says, to others for Me; a love not in word or in tongue, but in deed and in truth. Prove your love to Me by loving Mine. Feed My lambs, tend My flock. Take this child and nurse it for Me, care for this servant, this penitent: I will give thee thy reward.[1]

As we think of our Lord's Word addressed to His Friends, let us ask ourselves: (1) Are we faithful in our friendships—standing by them in adversity, like S. John? (2) Do we, like Jesus, recognize our friends and their service—not taking all for granted? (3) Do we expect to receive fresh duties from Him, and show ourselves ready to encourage, to support, and succor others?

Ps. xvi.
Collect, 2d for Good Friday.
Hymn, "By the Cross her station keeping."

---

[1] 1 S. John iii. 18; S. John xxi. 15–17; Ex. ii. 9.

IV.

OF SIN.

"My God, My God, why hast thou forsaken me?"—S. MATT. xxvii. 46.

WE pass from the regard of Persons to that of Things. Darkness now enshrouds the Cross. The sun hides his face from that dreadful sight. The outward gloom is but the shadow of a greater darkness which enveloped the human Soul of Jesus. Spirits of darkness crowd round for a final assault. Out of that darkness came the exceeding bitter cry, "My God, My God, why hast thou forsaken me?" Indeed the waters are come in. His soul is exceeding sorrowful, even unto death.

1. He has parted from His Friends. All external duties are fulfilled. Provision has been made for them. Now He has time and opportunity, if we may so say, to think, at least to speak, of Himself. S. John has led away the blessed Mother. Their presence had been a certain stay, even as He had asked His disciples in the Garden to watch with Him, relying to a certain extent on the support of their sympathy.[1] Now He is left alone. Hitherto He could always say, "Alone, yet not alone, for the Father is with Me."[2] But now the consciousness of

---

[1] S. Matt. xxvi. 38.   [2] S. John xvi. 32.

the Father's love seems to be withdrawn, His Face is veiled. This it is which is expressed in the bitter cry, "My God, My God, why hast thou forsaken me?"

2. Jesus is now tasting indeed the bitterness of death, the misery of sin. He is experiencing, so far as is possible, the sinner's doom. For what is that but the loss of God, Who is the soul's true satisfaction and stay? Man without God, when other things fail, being either withdrawn or used up—what is this but the very pain of Hell? The heart of man is made for God, and nought but God can fill it: it is ever restless until it find its rest in Him.[1] Jesus on the Cross is, in a sense, in the sinner's place—by the power of His sympathy, and as the representative of the fallen race. His cry of woe reveals the barrier which exists between sin and the Holy God, which necessarily shuts out the sinner, if he be not won, from God and happiness. Sin does separate, must separate from God. It is the contradiction of His every attribute. It is the wilful withdrawing from obedience to His will. Sin is the act of madness whereby man in his folly parts with God. Indeed it is an evil and bitter thing to forsake the fountain of living waters, and in our disobedience, our pride, sensuality, dishonesty, to hew out for ourselves cisterns, broken cisterns, that can hold no water.[2] We can understand something of the anguish of Jesus' soul expressed in this cry, if we

---

[1] S. Augustine's Confessions, I., 1.   [2] Jer. ii. 13, 19.

think of the agony of losing belief—some of you have known it clouded. What then is left? we ask; what to live for, what to hold by, what to cheer and guide?

The cry of Jesus tells us of sin chosen and sin found, of God rejected and God lost. It is, remember, no arbitrary hiding of His Face that we have to fear. Sin is a necessary, an inevitable barrier. We learn *God's regard of sin.* "Your iniquities," He says, "have separated between you and your God, and your sins have hid his face from you, that he will not hear. Therefore wash you, make you clean; put away the evil of your doings from before mine eyes; cease to do evil; learn to do well; seek judgment, relieve the oppressed, judge the fatherless, plead for the widow."[1]

3. And *man's true regard,* the true man's regard, of sin we learn. He hates it, dallies not with it, but treats it ever as an evil and abominable thing. God's commandments, he knows, are not grievous. All His statutes are for our good always.[2] Sin therefore he recognizes as folly.

Thus we understand something of the meaning of our Lord's cry. In His Passion He is a Penitent, the representative of fallen man. He is not punished as man's Substitute, but He sorrows as man's Representative. He tastes death, and the penalty of sin for every man.[3] By His penitence He would win all to penitence. Drinking into Himself, as it were, in the Cup of the Passion the tainted draught

---

[1] Isa. lix. 2; i. 16, 17.

[2] 1 S. John v. 3; Deut. vi. 24.   [3] Heb. ii. 9.

of man's polluted life, by a mighty act of contrition He diverts the course of human life, and pours forth from Himself in the Chalice of the Eucharist a stream of new, sanctified, and sanctifying life.

He is the Lamb of God that taketh away, by first taking on Himself, the sins of the world.[1] Both as Priest and Victim He is the sin-bearer.

> "Now the torrents of His Passion
>   Deep and fierce above Him roll;
> And the rivers of transgression
>   Overwhelm His Human Soul.
> Sins unknown, sins unimagined,
>   Sins by day and sins by night,
> Sins of blackest, outer darkness
>   Press upon His purest sight;
> Sins since o'er the Eastern portal
>   First the cherub waved his sword,
> Till the last that shall be written
>   Ere the coming of the Lord."[2]

As we contemplate His sorrow, the sorrow of His penitence, we will learn to sorrow for sin with a godly sorrow[3]—not for the loss of reputation it may have involved, nor for any temporal consequences we may suffer, but because of the offence to Almighty God. Considering His regard of sin we would arm ourselves likewise with the same mind.

   Ps. li.
   General Confession.
   Hymn, "O Sinner, lift the eye of faith."

---

[1] S. John i. 29; 1 S. Pet. ii. 24.
[2] Dr. Neale's Hymn for Maundy Thursday.
[3] 2 Cor. vii. 9–11.

V.

OF PAIN.

"I thirst."—S. JOHN xix. 28.

THESE last Four Words are like the ejaculations of a dying man. They are spoken at shorter intervals. The first three were more deliberate, spoken in the light. These are forced from our Lord, as it were, by the pressure of His woe. The Fourth Word is the expression of Spiritual Anguish, the Fifth of Bodily Torment. He was true Man, really tasting our sorrows. In *all* our afflictions He was afflicted —in the lesser as well as the greater. You know the feverish thirst which often accompanies the approach of death. In the death of crucifixion the thirst would be peculiarly intense, resulting in part from suffocation, and being aggravated by all our Lord had endured during the past night. He sympathizes with us in our *Pain*. He would show us how to regard Pain, how to meet it. From Him we would learn God's view of Pain, and man's true view.

1. It is not to be indiscriminately set aside.

When the procession arrived at the place of execution the soldiers had offered to our Lord, as to the other prisoners, the stupefying drug of wine mingled with myrrh, which was mercifully provided in all cases. The malefactors eagerly drank of it.

This accounts for the snatches of broken sentences, the wild cries which they uttered, as the intoxicating effect in part wore off. Jesus would not drink of it.[1] He would meet all, see all, bear all with unclouded faculties. *He refused the drug.* And herein gave an example to us. Not only with regard to anodynes and anæsthetics—certainly it is not unnecessary to warn of the great danger and wrong of their needless use—but with regard to softness and effeminacy in general. We seek to banish all sorrow, to distract ourselves from unpleasant thoughts. The penitential remembrance of sin is thought by some morbid. To tales and sounds of evil we close our eyes and ears. We will not think of them. We try to divert our minds from painful and disagreeable facts of life by the theatre and novels, or by idle business.

But Pain has an intended use. It is allowed for a purpose. Pain is a preservative. It is designed as a warning. We feel the burn that we may not be consumed.

In a world not constituted as ours is, Pain and Suffering might not be necessary. In our world we can see it is. It is a fact of experience, whether we can explain it or not, that suffering has a refining, ennobling, purifying effect. Without that check I might have drifted I know not whither; I was brought to my bearings by suffering. Those lines of beauty in the character I revere would not have

---

[1] S. Mark xv. 23.

been traced without that discipline. The bereavements, loss of fortune, failure of health, thwarting of plans, desertions—all that seemed so grievous— we could not afford to have done without them. Looking back we say, "It is good for me that I have been in trouble."[1] It has deepened my life, developed my character. As the outer man has decayed, the inner man has been renewed; the loss of earthly consolation has developed a deeper spiritual thirst, a hunger and thirst after righteousness.[2] So we learn to submit to sorrow, to accept discipline. Lord, Thou canst and wilt for me far better than for myself I either could or would.

Apart from argument we recognize suffering as the Royal Road, the way the King passed. His courtiers would follow Him. We pray Him by His Cross and Pain to hallow all suffering, to grant to all sufferers to use it rightly. Like every means of grace it requires right dispositions for its profitable reception.

2. At the same time there is another side to this consideration of suffering suggested by our Lord's Word from the Cross. See the perfect balance of His example. He says, "I thirst." He appeals for help. He accepts what one of the soldiers, moved with pity, offers—a taste of the sour wine brought for their own refreshment.[3] Christianity is not Stoicism.

---

[1] Ps. cxix. 67, 71.
[2] 2 Cor. iv. 16; S. Matt. v. 6; Isa. lv. 2.
[3] S. Mark xv. 36; S. John xix. 29.

We may accept lawful alleviations. We are bidden tend the sick and suffering, minister to Him in His needy members, to Him in them, to them for Him. Here is another gain of suffering. It gives opportunity for loving deeds. We look forward to the abolition of suffering when sin, from which it springs, shall be abolished. Then shall God wipe away every tear from every eye.[1] Meanwhile we do our part to alleviate suffering, to exterminate its cause.

    Ps. xli.
    Collect, 2d Sunday after Easter.
    Hymn, "O Sacred Head."

---

[1] Rev. xxi. 4.

VI.

OF WORK.

"It is finished."—S. JOHN xix. 30.

1. MAN goeth forth to his work and to his labor until the evening. The night cometh when no man can work. Therefore the Ideal Man so zealously set Himself to accomplish the *Work* committed to Him. I must work the works of Him that sent Me while it is day. Now He could say, "I have finished the work which thou gavest me to do."[1]

God has a work for all, for each of us to do; a work to do in our day and circumstances, with our gifts and opportunities; a work, whether it be great or little, for which we are fitted by His Wisdom, which reacheth from one end to another, mightily and sweetly ordering all things.[2] This work God intends to have an effect on us who do it. It matters comparatively little the mark we make on the world as we pass through it. The mark the world makes on us is of far greater importance. A Napoleon may redistribute the map of Europe; and the divisions may be wiped out like the castles children build on the sand by the returning tide. But the child has grown stronger by its exercise. And our character is developed by our work. Lines for good

---

[1] S. John ix. 4; xvii. 4.   [2] Wisd. viii. 1.

or evil are traced on our moral being, of ambition or of generous self-sacrifice. These marks we carry from stage to stage of life, from school to adult life, into the married state or the priesthood, aye, into the other world.

2. See the pattern of our Lord's Work, as the true Man, from first to last.

a. The *zeal and diligence* with which He undertakes it. "Lo, I come to do thy will." "My meat is to do the will of him that sent me, and to accomplish his work." So he enters on His ministry. "I have a baptism to be baptized with; and how am I straitened till it be accomplished!"[1]

b. At the same time *the discipline by which His work was regulated.* He restrains Himself until the appointed time, until He is thirty years of age. And then He sets His face like a flint, allowing nothing to divert Him, neither the interference of friends nor the dissuasion of enemies.[2]

c. His work is accomplished *in spite of every obstacle*—at any cost. Work will cost. In the sweat of thy brow shalt thou eat—and break—bread.

"Faint and weary Thou hast sought me,
On the Cross of suffering bought me."[3]

---

[1] Ps. xl. 9, 10; Heb. x. 7; S. John iv. 34; S. Luke xii. 50.

[2] S. Luke iii. 23; S. John ii. 4; S. Mark iii. 31–33; viii. 32, 33.

[3] S. John iv. 6; S. Mark iv. 38; Gen. iii. 19.

This is His cry:

> "I will ransom them from the power of the grave,
> I will redeem them from death:
> O death, I will be thy plagues,
> O grave, I will be thy destruction:
> Repentance shall be hid from mine eyes."[1]

d. His work is accomplished *in the midst of failure.* It is not success that He sets before Him, but faithfulness. When He gives an account of His ministry, "I have glorified thee on the earth," He says. How? "I have accomplished the work which thou gavest me to do. Of those whom thou gavest me, I have lost none, save the son of perdition." None through any fault of Mine, only him who would not be kept.[2] His obedience and faithfulness were manifested in the midst of external, seeming failure. The loud victorious cry, "It is finished," tells of His obedience even unto death, of His triumph over spiritual foes. The lust of the flesh, the lust of the eye, and the pride of life are trampled under foot. The Seed of the Woman has bruised the serpent's head at the expense of the bruising of His own heel in the combat.[3]

3. Can we echo our Lord's word? Have we so done, are we so doing, the work given to us, without and within?

Without, not self-chosen work, but the work marked out for us—in our family, in society, in busi-

---

[1] Hos. xiii. 14.   [2] S. John xvii. 4, 12.   [3] Gen. iii. 15.

ness employments, in deeds of charity, whether corporal or spiritual—patiently, perseveringly performing all such good works as God has prepared that we should walk in?

Within, fighting out temptations, seeking to bring every thought into captivity to the obedience of Christ; saying, "I will follow upon mine enemies and overtake them, neither will I turn again until I have destroyed them?"[1]

So would we arm ourselves with the same mind that was in Christ—not to do the same things, but to do whatever He appoints for us, after His example and in His spirit.

Ps. cxlii.

Collect in Order for Visitation of the Sick,

"Prayer which may be said in behalf of all present."

Hymn, Battle Song, "Jesus, Master, King of Glory."

---

[1] 2 Cor. x. 5; Ps. xviii. 37.

VII.

GOD'S REGARD OF MAN AND MAN'S OF GOD.

"Father, into thy hands I commend my spirit."—S. LUKE xxiii. 46.

WE have considered God's view and man's true view, the true Man's view, of Sinners, Penitents, Friends, of Sin, of Pain, of Work. There is not much else to view—saving one another. And this is what we have put before us, expressed in the last Word from the Cross—*God's view of man and man's view of God.*

1. God and man are at last at one again. The At-one-ment is effected. God has won man back to Himself. The estrangement was on man's side. God was yearning over His fallen creature, His prodigal son. He devised means that His banished should not be expelled from Him.[1] "God so loved the world, that he gave his Only begotten Son, that whosoever believeth in him should not perish, but should have eternal life.[2] The exhibition of God's love in the Incarnation and the Passion has *drawn man* with the cords of a man, with the bands of love, has softened man's heart.[3]

---
[1] 2 Sam. xiv. 14.   [2] S. John iii. 16.   [3] Hos. xi. 4.

Moreover, *redemption* from the power of evil, from the bondage of sin, has been effected. The bands are snapped; the foes trodden down. Jesus has made peace by the blood of His Cross.[1] So in the person of the Representative Man, the Second Adam, redeemed Humanity utters this word, "Father, into Thy hands I commend my spirit."

2. And God accepts man, his obedience proved, in this his Representative. "This," he says, "is My beloved Son, in Whom I am indeed well pleased."[2] God delights in this spotless offering of Christ, perfected through suffering; not in the suffering, but in the love which was willing to suffer, in the perfection which the discipline of suffering has brought about.[3] Pleading our oneness with Him, our Head and Leader, we pray:

> "Look, Father, look on His anointed Face,
>   And only look on us as found in Him;
> Look not on our misusings of Thy grace,
>   Our prayer so languid and our faith so dim;
> For lo, between our sins and their reward
>   We set the Passion of Thy Son our Lord."[4]

So does God regard man in Christ, reconciled by Him, "accepted in the Beloved." He has made reconciliation for iniquity, made an end of sin, brought in "everlasting righteousness."[5]

---

[1] Col. i. 20.   [2] S. Matt. iii. 17.   [3] Heb. ii. 10.
[4] Dr. Bright's Eucharistic Hymn, "And now, O Father, mindful of the love."
[5] Eph. i. 6; Dan. ix. 24.

"For a small moment have I forsaken thee;
But with great mercies will I gather thee.
In a little wrath I hid my face from thee for a moment;
But with everlasting kindness will I have mercy on thee,
Saith the Lord thy Redeemer." [1]

3. Man's regard of God, ours, must correspond with this. "My Beloved is mine, and I am His." [2] Man can again call God his *Father*, for he is ready to surrender himself in trustful, loving obedience as His son. Can we? For this we keep Good Friday. Without this Good Friday would be vain. It would be no *Good* Friday for us. We will then make this Word of Christ's our own. If we cannot do so now, we will fight it out, and put away whatever hinders. And then in this trustful surrender we will be at peace.

Come what may, joy or sorrow, success or failure, sickness or health, life or death—"Into Thy Hands I commend my spirit." I fled from Thee as a sinner; I commend myself to Thee as a penitent. "I commend my *spirit*"—my inmost being; when I have nothing else to commend, when all else is stripped from me—money, friends, earthly goods. Naked came I out of my mother's womb, and naked return I to my Father's hands. Only I return *conscious*. What awaits me I know not, care not; the employment of the intermediate state, the nature of the purification through which I hope there

---

[1] Isa. liv. 7, 8.   [2] Cant. ii. 16.

to be perfected for the fulness of His joy—I know not and care not. It is *my Father* Who will deal with me. "Father, into Thy hands I commend my spirit."

>Ps. xxxi. 1–6.
>Collect, 1st for Good Friday.
>Hymn, "The sun is sinking fast."

BY THE SAME AUTHOR.

Sermons and Tracts.

	Cts.
THE WORDS FROM AND TO THE CROSS, MEDITATIONS	60
GOSPEL WOES (Lent Lectures)	60
SELF DISCIPLINE, Lenten Addresses	25 and 60
MEDITATIONS ON THE LIFE OF S. JOHN THE EVANGELIST	25
THE SAINTLY LIFE, Notes for Meditation on the Epistle to the Philippians	25
CONCERNING CHRIST AND THE CHURCH, A Devotional Exposition of the Epistle to the Ephesians	60
MEDITATIONS ON THE CREED	50
" " LORD'S PRAYER	50
" " EXAMPLE OF THE PASSION	35
" " COLLECTS (1. Advent to Trinity)	60
" " " (2. Trinity Season and Saints' Days)	60
EXPOSITION OF THE GOSPEL CANTICLES	50
REASONABLE FAITH, Four Sermons on Fundamental Christian Doctrines	20
THE INSPIRATION OF HOLY SCRIPTURE	10
READING THE BIBLE	5
CATHOLIC not PROTESTANT nor ROMAN CATHOLIC	15
APOSTOLIC SUCCESSION	10
THE EUCHARISTIC SACRIFICE	10
CONFESSION	10
THE CHRISTIAN LAW CONCERNING MARRIAGE AND DIVORCE	10

PRAYERS FOR THE DEPARTED, 5c.; THE COMMUNION OF SAINTS, 5c.; CHRISTIAN FRIENDSHIP, 10c.; RETREATS, 5c.; FASTING COMMUNION, 5c.; HINTS FOR LENT, 5c.; FASTING, 5c.

Mission House of S. John the Evangelist, 44 Temple St., Boston, Mass.

www.ingramcontent.com/pod-product-compliance
Lightning Source LLC
Chambersburg PA
CBHW020226090426
42735CB00010B/1605